EXPECT AND EXPERIENCE MIRACLES

By Deacon Steve Greco

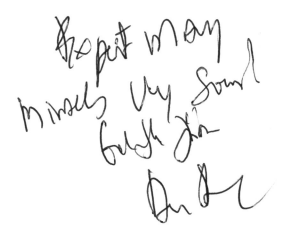

Dedication

This book is dedicated to all those who seek God with all their heart, soul, might and strength. He wants to show you His love. He wants to show you His miracles.

I also dedicate this book to my wife, Mary Anne, who has encouraged and supported me for more than 45 years. All my love forever!

Acknowledgements

I would like to thank the Spirit Filled Hearts Executive Team of my wife, Mary Anne; Michael Aimola, Vice President; and Katie Hughes, Director of Operations. I particularly want to thank Katie for her hard work on the book and the cover. I also thank my brother Bill Greco for his guidance.

One of the biggest gifts from the Lord was allowing Cindy Brauer to edit the book. Without her, I don't know where we would be. Her talent and expertise shines throughout the book! I can't thank you enough, Cindy, for editing and also for writing the Foreword!

CONTENTS

Foreword

God is not distant, serenely far away looking down on His creation. God is as close as our heartbeats. A God of intimacy. A God passionately in love with each of us. A God who fiercely wants us to know Him as He knows us — from the count of the hairs on our heads to the seconds of our lives.

That's the message to which my friend Deacon Steve Greco is now devoting his life. To spread the Good News of a loving, compassionate God, a God who holds us in the palm of His hand.

It is a calling for which Steve is uniquely qualified.

I have known Steve, his wife Mary Anne, and their family for nearly four decades. We have children about the same age and lived in the same neighborhood. We attended the same parish church and together were involved in youth ministry and other parish activities as well as youth sports, neighborhood events and the other myriad of events young and growing families encounter.

Steve and I also spent three years in Scripture study leadership classes, during which I received straight As on our assigned papers, besting Steve who earned all "As" but one — which he good-naturedly "laments" every time the occasion arises. Yet he was the one of us who emerged from those classes with a far deeper and more profound understanding and knowledge of the Bible.

Steve has always been a great speaker and motivator. In his professional life, those talents helped him reach the C-suite heights, leading sales departments at international pharmaceutical companies. He has also used these same gifts to serve God in his spiritual career as a leader in the Catholic Charismatic Renewal movement and a permanent ordained deacon for the Orange Diocese in Southern California.

Most recently, Steve and Mary Anne have been founders of the growing Spirit Filled Hearts Ministry, a faith group dedicated to spreading the Good News through the New Evangelization, building up the Church, teaching about the Holy Spirit and healing the Lord's people spiritually, emotionally and physically.

Steve gives talks and healing services throughout the United States in parishes and at Catholic conferences. He currently hosts a weekly radio show, "Empowered by the Spirit," heard on Immaculate Heart Radio. Clearly, he's a man with the gift and mission to preach!

This book, *Expect and Experience Miracles*, is drawn from one of Steve's presentations to Catholic groups in this country and abroad — one he considers the most important message he's been given to preach to all God's children. The book reflects Steve's grounding in Scripture and authentic desire to serve God by serving others.

Before listening to Steve's presentation on

expecting and experiencing miracles, I had a passing acquaintance with them, but really didn't consider direct divine interventions an integral part of my life. God has bigger miraculous fish to fry for really dire situations, perilous crises and truly deserving souls. I'm just a middle-aged woman with a good husband and four grown children simply trying to put one spiritual foot in front of the other on the faith journey of life.

But, as Steve testifies in this book, miracles aren't just for the "saintly or holy people." Miracles are meant for me and you — and the butcher, baker and candlestick maker, the postal carrier, late night diner fry cook, the star athlete, the computer whiz and the Fortune 500 CEO, the dog-walker and the space lab astronaut. Each and every one of us on God's beautiful blue marble of a planet are recipients of God's miracles.

And, as Steve tells us, some of these divine interventions are spectacular and jaw-dropping, while others are sweetly simple, but important at the moment (like making the green light when late for an important meeting). But big, small or medium in scope, each of us can expect and experience miracles if we have open hearts, faith and trust in God. Steve helps us do exactly that.

For his insights and enthusiastic encouragement, I thank him, and as Jesus would commend him:

> "Well done, my good and faithful servant." *Matthew 25:21*

Cindy Brauer, SFO
San Juan Capistrano, California
June, 2017

Introduction

I believe God passionately wanted me to write this book to give hope where hope is wanting. To increase faith, where little or no faith exists. And to shower you with His infinite and intense love.

We need only the faith of a little mustard seed to believe that our loving God wants to heal us and provide us miracles.

To God, miracles are simply His love in action — an everyday occurrence.

I am totally and completely convinced that God wants our faith to increase so that His miracles can flow "like a river." To renew the church. To transform lives. To bring a "New Pentecost" to the face of the earth.

What must we do to be agents of miracles? Nothing happens until we are ready to be used.

Are you ready? Do you want to be used? Will you live your purpose in life?

The first step always is to ask to be used. To passionately want to be used. To understand deeply. As Matthew's Gospel promises us, we need only to ask and we will receive.

> "Ask and it will be given to you; seek and you will find; knock and the door will be opened to you." *Matthew 7:7*

God uses us according to the depth of our passion to be used. He will send us to far places or next door to our neighbor for whatever He has in mind for us.

Most of us do not want to be inconvenienced. We want to be used only if it fits neatly into our schedule and doesn't make us too uncomfortable or embarrassed.

The words of Saint Paul in his letter to Timothy are as real today as in the first century — maybe even more now than ever.

> "Proclaim the word; be persistent

whether it is convenient or inconvenient; convince, reprimand, encourage through all patience and teaching." *2 Timothy 4:2*

Step out in faith. Remember Saint Mother Teresa's words, "God has not called us to be successful. God has called us to be faithful."

Don't be discouraged by what you see in the world. Memorize this verse from 2 Corinthians and live by it:

"For we walk by faith, not by sight."
2 Corinthians 5:7

Be relentless in pursuing miracles. As much as you want miracles to happen in your life or the lives of those you love and pray for, God wants even more to grant those miracles. When you do your part, He does His:

"Therefore I tell you, all that you ask for in prayer, believe you will receive it and it will be yours." *Mark 11:24*

How exciting to know God loves us with a love

passionate, pure and without conditions! In turn, we can spread that love to all those whom God puts in our paths. Our lives will never be the same again!

"Heavenly Father, we love you with all our hearts, souls, might and strength. Give us the courage to ask to be used as your agent of love and miracles. May we hunger and thirst to be used by you.

"Teach us how to expect miracles, through the power of the Holy Spirit, the intercession of the Sacred Heart of Jesus and the Immaculate Heart of Mary, in the name of Jesus our Lord and Savior, Amen."

My brothers and sisters, I love you with all my heart. I pray fervently for miracles for you and your family. I know God has touched you mightily, and you soon will expect and experience miracles every day of your lives.

Yours in Christ,
Deacon Steve

Part One

Looking for Miracles with the Holy Spirit's Help

Chapter 1
God's Miracles

We call them miracles — supernatural occurrences that enter our lives. The word comes from the Latin "to wonder." According to the *Catholic Encyclopedia*, miracles are "wonders performed by supernatural power as signs of some special mission or gift and explicitly ascribed to God." [1]

For God, miracles are love in action!

It is God's nature to love. To love each and every one of us passionately, completely and unconditionally. God wants us to know with faith that He is real. We see this in Hebrews:

> "But without faith it is impossible to please Him, for anyone who approaches God must believe that He exists and that He rewards those who seek him."

It is our choice, our response, to believe in God and His unending, unlimited love. When we do believe, we must also believe in His miracles.

The Bible is replete with signs and wonders. In the Gospel of John, for example, Jesus performs seven signs or wonders, including the raising of Lazarus and changing water into wine at the wedding feast in Cana. [2] All four Gospels tell of Jesus feeding thousands with just a few fish and loaves of bread. [3] Jesus walks on water.[4] In the Old Testament, Elijah receives comfort and instructions from God; [5] Moses crosses the Red Sea; [6] and Daniel is saved from the lion's jaws. [7]

In traveling to many places throughout the United States and the world, I often speak on miracles and ask people if they have experienced one or more of God's supernatural interventions in their lives. In almost every instance, people raise their hands and acknowledge that miracles have been present in their lives. When asked to describe these interventions, they have no explanation of how a healing took place or how an event occurred except through God's help. The more we have faith, the more God opens our eyes to see the truth of His love in our lives.

Miracles big and small occur each and every day, even in this chaotic, failing world – a father is cured of cancer, a child is born, the last parking spot opens up, a rainbow appears in the sky, an old friend calls just as you think of him, rain falls on parched dry earth, forgiveness blesses estranged friends and families, a blinding storm lifts suddenly to allow a flight home to visit a dying parent...

We must open both our hearts and minds to recognize miracles. We need to "expect and experience miracles!"

Often God uses us to make miracles happen; we become His catalysts on earth, revealing His love in action. In fact, Jesus was very clear, as John reports in his Gospel, that we will do greater works than those He performed.

"Amen, Amen, I say to you, whoever believes in me will do the works that I do, and will do works even greater than these because I am going to the Father. And whatever you ask in my name, I will do, so that the Father may be glorified in the Son." *John 14:12-13*

This is an incredible promise! We will do what Jesus did and more! Jesus laid hands on the sick and they recovered! Jesus drove out demons! Jesus performed countless works of love and mercy and kindness! We, too, in the name of Jesus, can be God's messengers of miracles.

Miracles strengthen us by helping us realize that God is with us — we are not alone. When we experience a miracle, even if we can't prove it scientifically, we are filled with hope, passion and the desire to spread the Good News of Jesus Christ: God loves us without limit; God is with us always; God is present to us in miracles.

1. *Catholic Encyclopedia*, (1907-1912), retrieved from
   http://www.catholic.org/encyclopedia
2. John 2:1-11, 4:46-54, 5:2-9,6:1-1, 9:1-41, 11:3, 6:16-21,
   9:1-41, 11:1-44.
3. Matthew 14:13-21, John 6:1-13, Mark 6:34-44,
   Luke 9:10-17
4. Matthew 14:22-33, Mark 6:45-52, John 6:16-21
5. 1 Kings 19
6. Exodus 14:10-31
7. Daniel 6:17-22

Chapter 2
The Love of the Father

The source of all miracles is love. All true love comes from God, for God is love.

"We have come to know and to believe the love that God has for us.

"God is love, and whoever remains in love remains in God, and God in him."
1 John 4:16

One of the biggest challenges in life is opening our hearts to God's love. I have found, in speaking to many people, they find it so much easier to believe that God loves other people unconditionally, passionately and without condemnation. However, they struggle to accept that God loves them. I am one of those people.

To open the door for miracles, we can meditate

on how much God truly loves us. Chapters in the Bible such as Romans 8, John 15 and Ephesians 1 are especially helpful for this mediation.

God is real. He wants to intervene in our lives through miracles, big and small, because he loves us passionately. Love is His greatest gift! He loves us unconditionally, completely and without compromise or reservation. We cannot earn this love or make it go away.

When we begin to understand we are loved completely and unconditionally, we begin to trust God. When we trust God, we can expect Him to intervene in our lives directly or through other people.

Healing comes through intense love, a love that leads to a greater faith in God's desire to heal us and give us miracles.

Every single day of our lives, I believe God is saying to each of us,

> "Because you are precious in my eyes / and glorious, and because I love you."

This call to believe and trust in God's love can be challenging for those whose relationships with their earthly fathers has lacked unconditional love or has been ruptured by the sin of abuse—mental, physical, emotional or sexual abuse.

But we cannot compare human actions to those of our heavenly Father, who is agape love: merciful, forgiving, encouraging and protecting. Through contemplative prayer, we can experience the love of a Father we could not imagine possible.

It is impossible for us to receive love unless we make the decision to open our heart to God. To receive the miracles God has in store for us, we must learn to receive God's love and give it to others.

"Whoever is without love does not know God, for God is love." *1 John 4:8*

God's love is vast and wise—He gives us what we need when we need it.

"My God will fully supply whatever you need, in accord with his glorious riches in Christ Jesus ." *Philippians 4:19*

The Father in heaven gives us supernatural strength to endure our trials. When we draw upon this strength, we can expect and experience miracles.

Chapter 3
Looking for Miracles

The Lord has come to me many times to say "Tell my people how much I love them. Tell my people that they are not alone and that I am with them. Tell my people that my Holy Spirit provides power, grace and love each day of their lives.

"Tell my people that miracles are there for them every single day, but they must look for them. They must expect them; they must want to experience my love."

Looking, seeing and recognizing miracles is fundamental to the growth of our faith.

The following story taught me, through the simple but profound faith of a child, how to look for miracles.

Miracle of the Rainbow

When my son Paul was about five years old, he came home one day from preschool as my wife Mary Anne was fixing dinner. Paul was one of those super-enthusiastic little boys, and he said, "Mom! Guess what? Jesus is going to give me a rainbow!"

It was late spring, soon to be summer, and we lived in Southern California where rain does not fall often during our dry summers. Mary Anne and I looked at each other thinking soon he would be distracted and forget all about rainbows.

Paul was in a special education program, and his language was limited. So we believed his teacher must have talked about rainbows to the class that day. A few days later, we happened to see the teacher, and we shared Paul's rainbow story. To our great surprise, the teacher said she hadn't spoken of rainbows in class.

We kept hoping Paul would forget Jesus' promise of a rainbow. But NOOOOOO! Every night he thanked Jesus for the rainbow. Although we continued to downplay the idea, we did search for any sign of a multicolored arc in the sky.

Mary Anne and I called each other if the tiniest hope of seeing a rainbow appeared...maybe that one cloud would produce a rainbow for Paul.

Day after day, we looked to the sky. No rainbow. Paul even said, "Jesus was going to give me the rainbow in two weeks." The pressure was really on! Our faith was being tested.

Paul's confidence in God must have been contagious. Mary Anne and I discovered a surprising peace in the knowledge that God was going to do something special for our little boy.

We continued to pray and praise God. Each day, Paul confidently thanked God for his rainbow. Soon, we would understand God's miracles can happen when and in ways we least expect.

That summer, we took a family vacation to Santa Barbara, renting an ocean-side cottage that boasted a large front lawn. One day, under a bright blue sky, Mary Anne, Paul and I stepped out onto the cottage porch.

Suddenly, on this cloudless day under an incredibly bright sun, rainbows appeared in the spray of every single sprinkler — 12 rainbows in all! Paul, with the biggest smile I have ever seen, turned to us and said, "Thank you, Jesus, for giving me my rainbows!"

At a time when Mary Anne and I were struggling with our own faith, the miracle of rainbows was a gift of faith for our son, and yes, a gift of faith for us!

God gives us our hearts' desires.

> "Find your delight in the LORD / who will give you your heart's desire."
> *Psalm 37:4*

One lesson we learned from the rainbow miracle is to remain vigilant and expect God will act in His time and in His way. Look for

God in all things and at all times. Paul's rainbows were low to the ground, as he was. The perfect location and size for his miracle!

Miracle of the Dolphins

No one outdoes God's grace, love and gifts. They happen in the perfect way and in the perfect time. We must have faith and never lose confidence or endurance to realize what God has planned for us.

> "Therefore, do not throw away your confidence; it will have great recompense. You need endurance to do the will of God and receive what he has promised." *Hebrews 10:35-36*

We often want to give up just when God is ready to allow the miracle to occur!

One day Mary Anne and I were at the beach, riding our bikes on the boardwalk. Mary Anne was in an uncharacteristically sad mood and I wanted to cheer her up. I said a quick prayer for God to bless her.

As we were riding, we came upon a school playground area not far from the ocean's edge. I asked Mary Anne to come with me to see the water, and I prayed asking God for a miracle. Mary Anne has a special love for dolphins, and I thought if God would show her a dolphin, her sadness would fade. So I quietly prayed and expected God to provide a miracle.

Many minutes went by and no dolphins. I kept looking for any sign of the sleek, graceful creatures among the ocean's waves. Mary Anne wanted to leave, but I said, "Let's wait a little longer."

Suddenly, not one, not two, not three or four, but <u>five</u> dolphins appeared in the distance swimming toward us! Mary Anne's face glowed with the biggest, most beautiful smile, and I thanked God for this miracle.

I looked behind me and saw many people on a crowded boardwalk, walking, running, biking, rollerblading, etc. No one had their eyes on the ocean to witness the miracle I believed had occurred. I asked the Lord why others didn't experience what I thought was a miracle. I then clearly understood that God gives a special grace to those who desire to see a miracle, and God allows them to experience miracles in His time.

Every single day of the week, I expect miracles. Every single day, I look around me and know that God loves me beyond anything I can possibly understand or imagine. God wants to fill me — and each one of us — with His love.

Noah's Miracle

In Scripture, the author of Hebrews recounts the story of Noah and the ark, offering an example of an incredible miracle and the faith essential to experience it.

> "By faith Noah, warned about what was not yet seen, with reverence built an ark for the salvation of his household. Through this he condemned the world and inherited the righteousness that comes through faith." *Hebrews 11:7*

Noah easily could have said no to the Lord's request to build an ark. If he had refused, he would have denied his family the miracle of surviving the flood.

He also would have said no to God's covenant.

> "I set my bow in the clouds to serve as a sign of the covenant between me and the earth. When I bring clouds over the earth, and the bow appears in the clouds, I will recall the covenant I have made between me and you and all living beings, so that the waters will never again become a flood to destroy all mortal beings. As the bow appears in the clouds, I will see it and recall the everlasting covenant between God and all living beings — all mortal creatures that are on earth." God told Noah, "This is the sign of the covenant I have established between me and all mortal creatures that are on earth."
>
> *Genesis 9:13-17*

Looking for miracles every day and trusting that our God is the God of miracles is a critical step in experiencing them routinely.

Chapter 4
The Purpose of Miracles

Why does God allow impactful and miraculous things to happen? So that, by faith, we know God is true and real. That we know God's compassionate, healing love. That we know God remains with us always and forever.

This fundamental knowledge is the cornerstone of experiencing miracles. Expecting miracles in our lives is faith in action.

One of the best Scripture examples of a faith that leads to miracles is the faith of the centurion in Matthew's Gospel.

> "When he entered Capernaum, a centurion approached him and appealed to him saying, 'Lord, my servant is lying at home paralyzed, suffering dreadfully.' He said to him, 'I

will come and cure him.' The centurion said in reply, 'Lord, I am not worthy to have you enter under my roof; only say the word and my servant will be healed. For I too am a person subject to authority with soldiers subject to me. And I say to one, "Go," and he goes; and to another "Come here," and he comes, and to my slave, "Do this," and he does it.' When Jesus heard this, he was amazed and said to those following him, 'Amen, I say to you, in no one in Israel have I found such faith.'...And Jesus said to the centurion, 'You may go; as you have believed, let it be done for you.' And at that very hour [his] servant was healed."   *Matthew 8: 5-10, 13*

The more faith we have, the more we understand miracles are everywhere, and we begin to expect them in everything. When God is the center of our lives, we realize He is constantly working miracles.

However, no matter how many miracles we may experience, we can quickly forget what God has done. We may begin to doubt and lose our trust in Him—that God can and will help us in our distress. Remembering our faith, we can again recognize that miracles are tools of love. They teach us of God's love, and they happen in God's way and in God's time.

When we allow our Lord to use us in His miracles, we will experience miraculous events on a routine basis. John's Gospel reminds that God chooses us.

> "It was not you who chose me, but I who chose you and appointed you to go and bear fruit that will remain, so that whatever you ask the Father in my name he may give you." *John 15:16*

I look for God's healing love every time I pray with someone. Many times, the primary purpose of the prayer is spiritual. Often it leads to physical healing.

A great example of God's healing love is Matthew's account of the paralytic.

> "And...people brought to him a paralytic lying on a stretcher. When Jesus saw their faith, he said to the

paralytic, 'Courage, child, your sins are forgiven…Which is easier, to say "Your sins are forgiven," or to say, "Rise and walk"? But that you may know that the Son of Man has authority on earth to forgive sins' — he then said to the paralytic, 'Rise, pick up your stretcher, and go home.' "   *Matthew 9: 2, 5-6*

When we pray over people and they are healed spiritually, mentally, emotionally or physically, that is a miracle. When we pray with someone and she turns to God through healing prayer, that is a miracle!

Amazingly, in the story of the paralytic, Jesus gives us instructions on how His miracles work. Jesus wants to heal us and he wants us to pray over the afflicted so they will recover. But Jesus first heals the paralytic spiritually, revealing that when we pray for the sick, the most important prayer is for their spiritual wellbeing.

The healing of God's people demonstrates His great compassion for each of us. God loves us so much and desires for us to live life fully and abundantly.

Do we choose to surrender to His love today and every day? Do we ask for His healing spiritually, emotionally, mentally and physically? Do we expect God will heal us and do we believe in His miracles? Praise God, now and forever!

Chapter 5
Holy Spirit Dynamite!

The book of Acts contains one of my favorite Scripture verses. Just before He ascends to heaven, Jesus promises the disciples He will not leave them alone.

> "But you will receive the power when the holy Spirit comes upon you, and you will be my witnesses in Jerusalem, throughout Judea and Samaria, and to the end of the earth."   *Acts 1:8*

It is the power of the promised Holy Spirit to which we turn in faith to expect and experience miracles.

The Greek word for power in Acts 1:8 is "*dunamis*," the root form of our English word "dynamite." The power of the Holy Spirit is explosive!

When we call upon the Holy Spirit, our lives as Christians explode with strength and dynamic power to conquer evil with the love of Christ, as Paul so clearly tells the people of Corinth.

"For the kingdom of God is not a matter of talk but of power."   *1 Corinthians 4:20*

Power against Fear

So many people are afraid—afraid of what might happen to them or their families, fearful in an often-violent world where God's love seems lost to so many. But fear stands for:

"<u>F</u>alse <u>E</u>vidence <u>A</u>ppearing <u>R</u>eal."

The devil is a liar and wants us to doubt our future destiny and present circumstances. Yet we need not fear anything! The dynamic power of the Holy Spirit is with us always, greater than any force we can imagine.

"You belong to God, children, and you have conquered them, for the one who is in you is greater than the one who is in the world."   *1 John 4:4*

Paul echoes this assurance in his letter to the Christians in Philippi.

> "I have the strength for everything through him who empowers me."
>
> *Philippians 4:13*

In traveling many places in the United Sates and the world, I have met so many people who believe they are alone and that God will not meet their needs. Nothing could be further from the truth! We see this clearly, again, in Philippians.

> "My God will fully supply whatever you need, in accord with his glorious riches in Christ Jesus."   *Philippians 4: 19*

The Holy Spirit's Powerful Gifts

Faith in the power of the Holy Spirit leads us to receive His many gifts and fruits. We receive His wisdom to make the right decisions, His courage to endure trials and hardships, the knowledge that we are not alone.

The New Testament mentions 27 gifts of the

Holy Spirit. 1 Corinthians 12 lists nine classical charismatic gifts: wisdom, word of knowledge, faith, healing, miracles, prophecy, discernment of spirits, tongues and interpretation of tongues. We are commissioned to use these gifts of the Holy Spirit in the work of the Church.

The Second Vatican Council's *Lumen Gentium*, *Dogmatic Constitution of the Church*, speaks of the charismatic gifts in paragraph 12.

> "...Whether they are the more outstanding or the more simple and widely diffused, they are to be received with thanksgiving and consolation, for they are exceedingly suitable and useful to the needs of the Church."

Each of us is blessed with particular gifts, as the Letter to the Romans teaches us.

> "For as in one body we have many parts, and all the parts do not have the same function, so we, though many, are one body in Christ and individually parts of one another. Since we have gifts

that differ according to the grace given

to us, let us exercise them: if prophecy, in proportion to the faith; if ministry, in ministering; if one is a teacher, in teaching; if one exhorts, in exhortation; if one contributes, in generosity; if one is over others, with diligence; if one does acts of mercy, with cheerfulness."

Romans 12: 4-8

But we need each other—all members of the body of Christ—to use our own gifts for the work of the Church as Paul reminds us in 1 Corinthians.

"To each individual the manifestation of the Spirit is given to some benefit."

1 Corinthians 12: 7

That is why prayer communities are so critical. It is through the gifts of the body of Christ that great miracles are manifested. Luke's description of the early Church clearly demonstrates the power of the Holy Spirit working in community.

"They devoted themselves to the teaching of the apostles and to the

communal life, to the breaking of the bread and to the prayers. Awe came upon everyone and many wonders and sign were done through the apostles."

Acts 2:42-43

What does this mean to us, Catholic Christians in the 21st century?

First, the sacramental life of Mass and the Eucharist in community is mandatory to receive the power and promises of Christ. Second, solid teaching is essential. So many Catholics live in partial, if not complete ignorance, of the power of the Holy Spirit. Finally, the faith of the community leads to boldness and boldness leads to releasing the Holy Spirit's power and miracles our lives.

The Holy Spirit's power makes the impossible possible! And that's dynamite!

Dynamite that will lead us to expect and experience miracles!

Chapter 6
Baptism of the Holy Spirit

Our invitation to accept the gifts of the Holy Spirit for the life of the Church begins the moment we are baptized, when we are anointed with sacred chrism on the crown of our heads. In that anointing, we are appointed priest, prophet and king. We are called to be God's servants in loving His people by proclaiming the Gospel, performing charity and using the gifts God provides us.

That is what being Catholic is all about! Jesus describes our purpose as Christians in Mark's Gospel.

"Go into the whole world and proclaim the gospel to every creature. Whoever believes and is baptized will be saved; whoever does not believe will be condemned. These signs will accompany those who believe: in my

name they will drive out demons, they will speak new languages. They will pick up serpents [with their hands], and if they drink any deadly thing, it will not harm them. They will lay hands on the sick, and they will recover."

Mark 16: 15-18

By receiving the grace of the power of the Holy Spirit, we have authority in Jesus to live out our purpose in life. In His name, we will "move mountains," proclaim his Good News and lay hands on the sick and they will recover. By living out our Christian purpose, we will see great miracles in our lives and the lives of others.

But living that purpose is no easy task as we face the challenges of a modern, secular society in which the enemy is attacking us in so many ways. Depression; addictions to drugs, alcohol, sex, video games; slavery to work, homosexuality and materialism are so commonplace—seen as normal by society in general.

However, we are not defenseless! The Holy

Spirit is our Advocate, our Defender, our Source of power. The power of God, the power of the Holy Spirit, in the name of Jesus, will be victorious over the challenges of contemporary life.

We receive the Holy Spirit's strength and gifts to allow Jesus to work through us. We perform the miracles needed to build the Church and to live a life of joy, love and abundance as promised in John's Gospel.

> "I came so that they might have life and have it more abundantly." *John 10:10b*

How do we get this abundant life? We must want it with all our hearts. We must ask for it as Jesus instructs us in Luke's Gospel.

> "And I tell you, ask and you receive; seek and you will find; knock and the door will be opened to you. For everyone who asks, receives; and the one who seeks, finds; and to the one who knocks, the door will be opened.

What father among you would hand his
son a snake when he asks for a fish? Or

hand him a scorpion when he asks for
an egg? If you then, who are wicked,
know how to give good gifts to your
children, how much more will the
Father in heaven give the holy Spirit to
those who ask him?"   *Luke 11: 9-13*

We must want the Holy Spirit. We must ask,
seek, and knock for the Holy Spirit to enter our
lives in a powerful way. When we do, then we
are "Baptized in the Holy Spirit."

A few years ago, I prayed for the Baptism of the
Holy Spirit over 150-plus children, ages 7-12, at
the Southern California Renewal Convention
(SCRC) on a Saturday in Anaheim, California.

The next day, on Sunday morning, I was
walking across the arena and a mother and her
daughter came running up to me.

"Deacon, Deacon, my daughter has something
she would like to ask you," said the mother.
"What is it?" I asked.

The daughter, with big brown eyes looking up

at me, said, "Did I receive the Holy Spirit at Baptism?"
I answered, "Excellent! I am very proud of you!"

Then the little girl, with a look on her face I will never forget, her eyes wide with wonderment, said something so wise, so profound that I think about her words almost daily.

"If I received the Holy Spirit at Baptism, then why is He hiding?"

Wow!!!! Is the Holy Spirit hiding in your life? Have you given the Holy Spirit the authority to be released in your life and do you manifest the gifts of the Holy Spirit? Do you pray, "Enkindle in me the fire of your love?"

Fire, power, purpose, love, joy and peace are the essence of a Christian's life. When you have that, you can expect and experience miracle

Chapter 7
Tools of the Holy Spirit

By accepting the gifts of the Holy Spirit, we fill our spiritual "toolbox" with powerful resources to experience miracles. The gift of tongues is especially important because it often initiates the other gifts of the Spirit.

I have been a charismatic prayer group leader since 1978. Yes, if you are doing the math that makes me, well, older...

We were young, my wife and I, just 28 years old, and full of the Holy Spirit. We were asked to take over a thriving Charismatic Renewal prayer group at a nearby parish. The group's members numbered about 40, mostly women, and Mary Anne and I were the youngest by far.

Supported by expert mentoring, I led the group's meetings while Mary Anne provided music, playing her guitar. We met Monday

mornings about 9 a.m. after Mass.

Through the Holy Spirit's gentle nudging, we were prompted to look for more ways to enliven the group meetings, to help members — and ourselves — to grow ever closer to God.

We realized for our prayer group to grow, to experience the love of Christ and the power of the Holy Spirit, the charismatic gifts must be manifested by the group's members.

Over the years, we came to understand prayer group members should and must yield to the charismatic gifts and use them with great power.

For example, I believe we do not use the gift of tongues to the level needed. In the last nearly 40 years, I have seen a significant downward trend in the use of the gift of tongues. It is important to realize that using the gift of tongues gives us the strength to pray for prophecy, healing and miracles.

In our prayer group during the praise and worship part of the meeting, we try to use the

gift of tongues for an entire hour before we pray over people. We have found the healing that occurs — spiritual mental, emotional and physical — is tremendously enhanced when the majority of the community is praying fervently in the Spirit.

Some people say they don't think the gift of tongues is very important or its use ended at the time of the Apostles. Why would Jesus stop such an important gift to us? He has not. If fact, it is estimated that millions of people in the world today pray in the Spirit, including many of the leaders of the Catholic Church.

Another important resource in our spiritual toolbox is healing prayer. Why don't people pray for healing more often? We are reassured of this power in Mark's Gospel.

> "They will lay hands on the sick, and
> they will recover."   *Mark 16:18b*

I have seen miracles brought about by healing

prayer over and over in three-plus decades.

One day at a local church, a friend of mine

asked me to pray over him after Mass. We went over to a statue of the Blessed Mother since my friend had a strong devotion to Mary. He told me doctors had found a cancerous mass in his lung, and he was given a 1-in-500 chance of survival.

All I could think about was how much Jesus loved my friend and how much the Blessed Mother loved him. I thought of the scripture verse from John's Gospel in which Jesus promised we would do what He did and more. I remembered the teaching that when two or more agree upon anything in Jesus' name, it shall be done.

> "Again, [amen,] I say to you, if two of you agree on earth about anything for which they are to pray, it shall be granted to them by my heavenly Father," *Matthew 18:19*

I prayed according to the direction in Mark's

Gospel.

> "Therefore I tell you, all that you ask for
> in prayer, believe that you will receive it
> and it shall be yours." *Mark 11:24*

I stood and prayed and believed. I called upon
the Blessed Mother to intercede with her Son on
behalf of my friend. I prayed in faith for his
healing through the power of the Holy Spirit in
the name of Jesus.

As I laid hands on him, he told me he felt fire
literally flowing through his chest and body
and down to his feet. He could hardly believe
the strength of this sensation. But he did believe
in the power and love of Jesus and the love of
his spiritual mother.

A week later, my friend had more tests done.
The oncologist couldn't believe it. Not a trace of
cancer was found! This happened more than
seven years ago, and the cancer has not
returned.

God is so good! We must believe!
Still another key resource in experiencing

miracles is the gift of great faith.

In Matthew's Gospel, we learn this critical
lesson in experiencing miracles.

> "And as Jesus passed on from there, two
> blind men followed [him], crying out,
> 'Son of David, have pity on us!' When
> he entered the house, the blind men
> approached him and Jesus said to them,
> 'Do you believe that I can do this?' 'Yes
> Lord,' they said to him. Then he touched
> their eyes and said, 'Let it be done for
> you according to your faith.' " *Matthew 9:
> 27-29*

Do you believe that God can heal you? Do you
truly believe? Or do you think that other people
can be healed, but not you? You are too sinful?
Not good enough? Not loved enough?

Another miracle example of using the tools of
the Holy Spirit occurred on one of the
pilgrimages Mary Anne and I have led to the
Holy Land. A member of the pilgrimage had
recently dislocated her shoulder. She could

barely move her arm, let alone lift it. The Lord gave me a "word of knowledge" as recounted in 1 Corinthians.

"...to another [is given] the expression of knowledge according to the same Spirit." *1 Corinthians 12:8*

That word was that God wanted to heal her shoulder.
I asked the woman if she believed that Jesus could heal her. I will forever remember her answer. She looked at me, her eyes wide open, and said with great passion, "I believe!"

I prayed over her and within 30 seconds she began thrusting her healed arm and shoulder into the air proclaiming, "Alleluia, Alleluia, Alleluia!" She praised God with all her heart the entire trip!

Wow!!!! Even though I have prayed and experienced countless miracles over the course of three decades, each time a miracle occurs, I am filled with wonder and awe. How good is our God!

My brothers and sisters, God is real. Jesus is real. Healing is real. We must believe and not be defeated by what we see with our human eyes. We must have faith:

> "For we walk by faith, not by sight."
> *2 Corinthians 5:7*

Don't believe the whisper in your ear from the enemy. Walk in faith! The tools of the Holy Spirit are so powerful, we can't help but expect and experience miracles!

Part Two

Essentials Elements for Miracles

Chapter 8
Five Keys to Miracles

Who does not want miracles in their lives? Who does not want to know God's love, power and grace?

Why do some people seem to experience nonstop miracles in their lives and most others never see or experience miraculous events?

There are five keys to experience miracles: surrender, request faith, fervent prayer, ask for miracles and forgive.

1. **Surrender.** We must give our lives completely to Jesus. In the Book of Revelation to the church of Laodicea we are told:

    > "I know your works; I know that you are neither cold nor hot... So, because you are lukewarm,

neither hot nor cold, I will spit

you out of my mouth."

Revelation 3:15-16

When we surrender, we put Jesus first in all that we do.

"But seek first the kingdom [of God] and his righteousness, and all these things will be given you besides."

Matthew 6:33

Put God first and it is the beginning of opening your heart to miracles.

2. **Request Faith.** When we ask for faith, we will get it. We see this not only in Luke's Gospel when we are instructed to ask, seek and receive (*Luke 11:9-13*), but throughout the New Testament. When we receive the faith for which we ask, we can move mountains.

"If you have faith the size of a mustard seed, you will say to this mountain, 'Move from here to there,' and it will move.

Nothing will be impossible for you." *Matthew 17:20*

Faith changes things. Most people who pray doubt that anything miraculous will happen.

3. **Fervent prayer.** The most important prayer we can ever make is fervent prayer, becoming one with God through prayer.

Fervent prayer reaches within our hearts to experience God so that we can unite with God through the power of the Holy Spirit.

Fervent prayer is praying with God in our hearts and not just with our human intellect. The most difficult journey is 18 inches from our heads to our hearts.

When we pray fervently with our hearts, our hopes turn into realities.

It matters not the length or kind of prayer, but only that we pray with a

fervent love of God, desiring only to be one with Him.

The thief on the cross and the centurion are two great examples of miracles occurring through fervent prayer. The Letter of James reminds us:

> "The fervent prayer of a righteous person is very powerful." *James 5:16*

4. **Ask for miracles.** We know that we must ask to receive and to seek in order to find. As James also admonishes us:

> "You do not possess because you do not ask. You ask but do not receive, because you ask wrongly, to spend it on your passions." *James 4:2b-3*

By asking for God's intervention in our lives each day, we are asking for miracles.

5. **Forgive.** I have been praying for healing

in the name of Jesus for 39 years. The fervent prayers of those who open their hearts to ask for miracles in faith are answered in the way that Jesus wants to heal them.

Besides lack of faith, the single biggest obstacle to answered prayer is lack of forgiveness. Mark's Gospel clearly instructs us:

> "When you stand to pray, forgive anyone against whom you have a grievance, so that your heavenly Father may in turn forgive your transgressions." *Mark 11:25*

As Mark indicates, it is essential that we seek forgiveness for our sins — including our own lack of forgiveness — in the Sacrament of Reconciliation.

Thus forgiven, we enhance our ability to be open to miracles.

Chapter 9
Surrender and Ask for Faith

Surrender is the first essential step in learning to expect and experience miracles. To help in this process, we meditate on the reality of how much God loves us. God wants so much for us to believe in Him, to know Him as a child knows their mother and father.

Faith in this loving God leads to wonderful things.

> "But without faith it is impossible to please him, for anyone who approaches God must believe that he exists and that he rewards those who seek him."
> *Hebrews 11:6*

Total and Complete Surrender

What is the key to experiencing this faith that

"passes all understanding?" It is total and

complete surrender. God desires all of us: our hearts, dreams, worries — everything!

When I was 28 years old, I was a District Sales Manager for a pharmaceutical company. A sales representative in the company was Catholic, but was very much in the world. One day he appeared at work wearing a "Holy Spirit" pin on his suit.

I looked at him and said, "What is this? Catholics don't wear Holy Spirit pins!"

He replied, "I found Jesus."

I looked at him in shock and replied, "You go to Mass every week, receive the Eucharist and listen to the readings; how can you say you just found Jesus?"

He said, "I never knew Him, His love and forgiveness."

I came home from work thinking about what he said. Did I truly know Jesus? If you followed me around all week could you convict me of being devoted to God? In what I said? What I

did? In my actions, thoughts and words?
I was active in my parish. I taught religious education, worked with the poor and attended Mass every week. Yet, something was missing. My friend had a conviction I did not have. He had a joy that I did not have.

That day, I made a decision. I would give my heart and soul to Jesus.

I looked at myself in the mirror in my bedroom and I said, "Jesus, take over my life, completely and totally."

And I meant it!

At that point, everything changed. I began praying in "tongues," although I didn't even know what that was. I went into my living room and saw a big, thick, dusty book that contained text and beautiful pictures. What was it? A Bible, of course. Sitting there, looking as if I actually read it. The reality is, I had rarely, if ever, opened this holy book!

I begin reading the Bible, and the words leapt off the pages. It was a love letter to me! A love

letter that told me I was forgiven. I was a child of God. I was not condemned, and <u>nothing</u> would separate me from the love of Christ. Wow! Why hadn't I known this before then?

I couldn't stop reading the Bible. Memorizing it. Quoting it. I spent literally an average of eight hours a day examining, pondering and praying over the words, messages and wisdom of the Bible.

I started quoting Scripture to everyone I encountered, at first, primarily my family and friends. They thought I was nuts! I realize now this awakening of mind and heart is what we call the "Baptism of the Holy Spirit." A Baptism of fire! Of love! Of joy! Of zeal!

I remember my mother's response.

"Catholics," she said, "don't quote scripture!"

Then, she couldn't handle it anymore.

"I know you have joined a cult," she said to me. "Come clean and tell me!"

I thought she was then going to ask me to describe the color of the "Kool Aid" I drank!

My mother decided that a solution to this sudden unusual behavior of mine was for me to visit a family relative who was a priest. When I met with him, he asked a lot of questions and finally decided I was probably okay, but I should read books on the saints.

However, something deeply profound had changed within me when I surrendered my complete being to God. The fire of the Holy Spirit was enkindled and began to blaze. And the zeal I have for the Lord and Scripture has only increased over time! Perhaps I am more tactful in expressing my faith, but the desire remains aflame.

When we surrender to the Lord, everything changes. We begin building the foundation of an abundant life and a life of miracles.

Jesus fervently wants us to live this abundant life, to trust Him and to embrace His passionate love for us. In John's Gospel, He tells us,

> "I came so that they might have life and
> have it more abundantly." *John 10:10*

We were created and designed to give our heart to Jesus!

We do that by totally surrendering to Jesus through the power of the Holy Spirit! Let us lift up our hands to our Heavenly Father with this prayer of surrender.

We pray:

"Heavenly Father I surrender my life to you, I surrender my soul to you. I surrender my dreams to you. Use me in any way you want. I love you. In Jesus' name. AMEN!"

Ask for Faith

Faith is a gift from our loving God; we don't earn it. We desire and request faith. Paul's letter to the Hebrews explains the importance of faith.

> "But without faith it is impossible to please him, for anyone who
>
> approaches God must believe that he exists and that he rewards those who seek him."
> *Hebrews 11:6*

We must ask for the power of faith. When we ask for an increase of faith with a pure and sincere heart, we can expect to receive it. All I want is to be a vessel for Jesus, but I need faith to step out to make a difference. The Gospel of Mark teaches us about faith.

> "Therefore I tell you, all that you ask for in prayer, believe that you will receive it and it will be yours."
> *Mark 11:24*

We <u>will</u> receive it!

Often people wonder why all their prayers are not answered. The First Letter of John explains why.

"And we have this confidence in him, that if we ask anything, he hears us. And if we know that he hears us in regard to whatever we ask, we know that what we have asked him for is ours."

1 John 5:14-15

We must ask in His will. So how does that work? We know God always hears prayer — 100 percent of the time.

We also know something else: good things and blessings will occur when we pray. Every time we pray!

With a pure heart, we can ask for an increase of faith and expect to get it.

If we pray over someone in fervent belief, healing does take place. However, the type of healing may be different than what we have asked. It might be spiritual, emotional or physical healing.

When we pray, God answers by "Yes" or "No" (meaning something better is in store!). Often the answer is "Not Yet" — there will be some time before our request is fulfilled — all according to God's time and will.

Something good will always happen when we surrender to God and trust in the gift of faith!

Chapter 10
Forgive and Expect Miracles

Most people wonder why we don't encounter miracles in our lives. As already discussed, we must first surrender our whole selves to God. If we haven't truly surrendered, we are praying in <u>our</u> will and not the will of the Father, as James clearly describes in his letter:

> "You ask but do not receive, because you ask wrongly, to spend it on your passions." *James 4:3*

I have found that when we surrender our lives to God, we realize the importance of forgiveness.

When we forgive others and ourselves, we then truly become ambassadors for Christ.

"So we are ambassadors for Christ, as

if God were appealing through us. We

implore you on behalf of Christ, be
reconciled to God." *2 Corinthians 5:20*

Forgiveness

To experience miracles, we must have a
forgiving hearts.

When we lack forgiveness, the grudges and
bitterness we hold toward those who have hurt
us become a poison that blocks the power of the
Lord. Without forgiveness in our hearts, trying
to pray feels very much like praying against a
brick wall.

Because so many of us struggle mightily with
mercy and reconciliation, forgiveness is a
critical part of our ministry. We ask people to
examine their consciences. Whom have they
not forgiven?

Many people simply want to block out painful
memories of those who have hurt them — even
those no longer living. Yet, reconciliation with
relatives — especially parents — or friends who

have passed, is so important for our spiritual health.

Don't fall into the trap of allowing painful hurts — real and perceived — to fester in your hearts and souls. Let the Lord heal your memories. Look at the people who have hurt you, living or dead, through the eyes of the Lord. Ask the Lord to help empty your heart of bitterness and anger so that you are ready to receive His gifts and miracles.

A forgiving heart is critically important for our spiritual health and to secure answers to our prayers!

Expect Miracles

Another essential component to experiencing miracles is so basic a concept, it could be taken for granted. We must learn to expect miracles! Believe God wants to intervene in our lives through tangible wonders and signs.

Many people believe miracles happened at the time of Jesus, but not today. Or they may accept miraculous events happen to the saintly or extremely holy person, but not to us struggling Christians.

I see and feel the disbelief when I pray for those who doubt. Often I see it in their eyes. They thank me for the prayers, but clearly don't think anything will happen as a result.

Those who doubt may simply and sincerely ask the Lord for increased faith and to understand how much we are loved by Him.

We believe and expect that God intends to shower us with grace. A favorite Scripture verse from Ephesians expresses this expectation.

> "Blessed be the God and Father of our Lord Jesus Christ, who has blessed us in Christ with every spiritual blessing in the heavens." *Ephesians 1:3*

Wow! Every spiritual blessing. But first, we must believe, trust and expect.

We don't know why God heals in certain ways

and in His timing. However, we do know how to remove the obstacles that hinder miracles: surrender, forgive and expect! Then we truly can experience miracles

Chapter 11
Expect Miracles in Your Family.

God is love. Where there is love, there is God. Where there is great love, with our families and those closest to us, I have found great miracles often occur.

With love, we can be pure of heart, leading us to serve as ambassadors of Christ with family and friends.

In praying for families, we can begin with our spouses, prayer enhanced by the Sacrament of Marriage.

My wife, Mary Anne, had severe arthritis in her hands and couldn't pick up anything without pain. She was on 16 pills a day. I prayed over her and believed each day; months later, she was completely healed! The doctor couldn't believe it!

Like most of you, Mary Anne and I have had our challenges with our children — spiritually, emotionally, mentally and physically. Praying fervently to God has brought one miracle after another.

We prayed for our daughter to marry a holy man. And she married a man we think is a saint in the making. He wasn't Catholic when they married, but years later converted and now he is, in many ways, an evangelist!

He has been amazing in supporting my daughter. As I write this book, my daughter is battling stage-four lung cancer. For strength, we stand on a verse from Romans.

> "We know that all things work for good for those who love God, who are called according to his purpose." *Romans 8:28*

Both our daughter and son-in-law have become "evangelists" for lung cancer research, appearing in print media and on radio and television shows. Our daughter volunteers with the U.S. Department of Defense to provide her perspective as a patient to aid in research.

Praise God!

My oldest son is an attorney who defends the poor, and my youngest son works for the Catholic Charismatic Renewal in the Archdiocese of Los Angeles. They both are doing amazing things!

What is the key? Faith, prayer and not giving up. The Letter to the Hebrews offers important instruction on persevering. I suggest committing these verses to memory, to recall during discouraging times:

> "Therefore, do not throw away your confidence; it will have great recompense. You need endurance to do the will of God and receive what he has promised."
>
> *Hebrews 10: 35-36*

One of the most powerful tools of miracles for families is the rosary. When my children were teenagers, I felt everything I did was wrong. I said "Green," and they said "Red, blue and white!"

One day when I was totally beside myself, I went into a church midday alone and prayed fervently. The Lord came upon me and said, "Pray the rosary every day for your family and children."

I haven't missed in nearly 30 years!

Never give up expecting miracles for your families, no matter the circumstances. For example, I experienced an example of the power of miracles and prayer a few years ago when I was preaching on the power of the Holy Spirit. A family of five approached me after the talk and asked for me to pray for their daughter who was in attendance.

The father told me the story. A senior in high school, their daughter had always had a devout faith and served as a leader in the local Catholic youth group.

One day, however, she stopped going to church. She became depressed and didn't want to leave her room. She even spoke of ending her life.

I asked the parents to join me in laying hands on their daughter and I expected a miracle. Suddenly, the Lord came upon me and I saw a vision of something evil buried in a chest of drawers in her room. I asked her parents to search the chest when they got home.

Later that night I received a text of a picture of a demonic tarot card. I told them to burn it immediately, which they did.

Within 24 hours, the young woman was completely back to normal. Praise God, now and forever!

God wants to heal your families today. He asks for your faith and to expect and experience His miracles.

Chapter 12
The Love of the Blessed Mother

How blessed are we that we have the love of the Blessed Mother! We have a spiritual mother who intercedes for us with her Son, just as she did at the wedding feast in Cana.

John's Gospel speaks of the special relationship we have with Mary when he recounts one of Jesus' last actions as he was dying on the cross.

> "When Jesus saw his mother and the disciple there whom he loved, he said to his mother, 'Woman behold your son.' Then he said to the disciple, 'Behold, your mother.' And from that hour the disciple took her into his home." *John 19:26-27*

My grandmother, Carmella, prayed the rosary every day and during Mass on Sunday.

Growing up, I observed how peaceful she was

when she prayed, but I did not have a devotion to Mary until later in life.

When our children were teenagers, and it seemed as if I couldn't do anything right, I went to church one day to pray. I asked the Lord to give me direction to raise my children and to be a good parent.

God's message was loud and clear. "Pray the rosary daily, plus a decade for each child." I have never missed a day!

The Blessed Mother wants to intercede through her Son to give us miracles. This belief was very obvious to me during an intense prayer session I had one Friday evening.

Four of us, my wife and two close friends—another married couple—had been praying for four hours that evening when God called me to pray over a woman who had a deep need for inner healing from her childhood.

As I began pray, I felt intense love for this

woman from God the Father. I asked that His love flow through me into the woman and heal

her memories.

Suddenly the miracle occurred! I saw the Blessed Mother standing just five feet away, dressed in a blue garment with a white stripe down the side and 12 stars encircling her head.

Instantly, I saw three angels kneeling by her. Then the entire room lit up, and many more angels appeared. The Blessed Mother lips were moving, and I could tell she was praying for the woman and all of us!

I cried out, "The Blessed Mother is here!"

We all started weeping in joy!

Through this amazing experience I realized the existence of a spiritual realm, hidden from us, in which the Blessed Mother, angels and saints are interceding for us!

The encounter changed my life; I truly understood we are not alone. When we call upon the communion of saints, we are not disappointed, even if we don't see them praying for us in our present reality.

During this same time, I felt God calling me to France to visit Paris and Lourdes. In Paris, I received another Marian miracle.

The Church of the Miraculous Medal is located on a street called Rue de Blanc. I was led to pray in that church at the Communion rail, to meditate on the Blessed Mother.

Initially, my mind went blank, but then I heard a voice in my head.

"I will give you the gift of poverty."

Wow! I knew that voice couldn't be my voice! I didn't want poverty! I was so disturbed that I ran, shaking, to the back of the church and entered into the last pew. I remember looking up and asking God, "Can we talk about this?"

Pondering the message, I realized I didn't want to be like the rich young man who didn't want to do what it took to follow Jesus in Mark's

Gospel (10:17-25). I slowly walked to the front of the church and told the Lord, "Take whatever you need to build up me and the church."

On the way back and when I returned home, the Lord revealed much more to me. He showed me the verse from Matthew:

> "Blessed are the poor in spirit, / for theirs is the kingdom of heaven."
> *Matthew 5:3*

God revealed to me that "poverty in spirit" means putting God first in all things. Matthew's Gospel says it succinctly.

> "But seek first the kingdom [of God] and his righteousness, and all these things will be given to you besides."
> *Matthew 6:33*

I recognized that I had made many things my gods. My family with everyone getting along perfectly. Sunday afternoon dinner. Success in business. My health. So many things.

What happened following this time of self-realization?

My family had a major blow-up. Half the family stopped talking to the other half. Not

only was Sunday dinner off the table, but also being together for holidays.

My good health was taken away; my back hurt with pains shooting down the side of my leg to my feet. Sciatica. I hadn't even known what the word meant.

For six months, I could barely stand for more than 30 seconds without severe pain. I went to one doctor after another, one treatment after another, before I found a pain specialist who helped me.

I got fired from my job. One day, I was Senior Vice President of a major pharmaceutical company, the next, out in the street with no job.

Ironically, I had recently been honored as one of the top executives in the company, told I was a "corporate treasure." I was fired two months later when senior management changed.

God's miracle, through what I believe was the voice of the Blessed Mother, was to show me that we need to trust God in the midst of all trials.

He will turn trials into good when we trust in Him and believe in His healing power. I now believe these difficult events in my life was God preparing me for the Diaconate program in our diocese. During that time, I had entered into the program's four-plus years of formation.

When we pray with our Blessed Mother and ask her to intercede for us with Jesus, we can expect and experience miracles!

Chapter 13
The Importance of Praise

Praise changes things. Praise changes everything!

Christian praise recognizes God's myriad attributes. Who is God? He is Love! He is the Prince of Peace, the Alpha and the Omega! He is the King of Kings and the Lord of Lords! He is our Deliverer, our Savior, our Redeemer! Our Healer! The Morning Star! Our Comforter and Advocate! The God of Mercy! The God of Hope! Our Creator! The Word made Flesh! Our Rock!

We were born to praise God.

> "The people whom I formed for myself,
> / that they might announce my praise."
> *Isaiah 43:21*

"Let everything that has breath / give

praise to the LORD!" *Psalm 150:6*

"Through him [then] let us continually offer God a sacrifice of praise, that is, the fruit of lips that confess his name."
Hebrews 13: 15-16

To experience God's miracles often and routinely, we must truly learn how to praise. Life will never be the same again!

I believe it is difficult, if not impossible, to be depressed or discouraged or to experience other emotion when we praise God. In praising God, we are transformed into His image. We receive His peace. We grow in our love for Jesus until our life becomes a reflection of He who is Love.

When praying for miracles, I always begin with praise and praying in tongues or "in the Spirit." This practice leads to the many types of miracles discussed in this book.

When in a crisis situation, try praise as a

solution and an entry to miracles. For example:

October 17, 1989, 5:04 p.m. Candlestick Park in San Francisco. A World Series game between the San Francisco Giants and Oakland Athletics.

A friend had gotten us great seats. At that very moment, a 7.1 earthquake hit. I thought the stadium structure was literally coming down around us, it rocked so badly. My friend and I determined how serious the situation was, then left the ballpark, heading to San Jose Airport, barely open 40 miles away.

I began praising God fervently, trusting in His love. Only one flight for Southern California was scheduled, and I had to be on it! I praised God fervently for His grace and miracles.

Despite not having a ticket on the flight, God allowed me to get on it! After I was seated, I heard over the intercom on the plane, "Would Steve Greco please come to the front of the plane?"

The request was indeed strange, since the

airline didn't have my name. What was up? I began praising God even more!

Arriving near the plane's cockpit, the flight attendant told me my friend Ray had contacted my wife, told her I was okay and to pick me up at Ontario airport. Praise God! Now and forever!

I have learned when we praise God, we can expect and experience miracles!

Part Three

God's Variety of Miracles

Chapter 14
Spiritual Miracles

The Lord's number one priority in healing creating miracles is our spiritual health.

We know this from the Bible's healing stories, particularly the story of the paralytic's miraculous cure, found in the Gospels of Matthew (9:1-8), Mark (2:1-12) and Luke (5:17-26). In these narratives, Jesus first tells the stricken young man, "Your sins are forgiven." Only then does Jesus heal him of his paralysis.

So many people live in spiritual darkness. They may go to church, but they struggle to believe in God or God's love. Our first task as Christ's ambassadors is to love them fervently and tell them they are loved unconditionally.

As the Letter of James tell us:

"Fervent prayer of a righteous person is

very powerful." *James 5:16*

Praying fervently for spiritual healing is greatly enhanced by living the fourth Beatitude.

"Blessed are those who hunger and thirst for righteousness / for they will be satisfied." *Matthew 5:6*

What does hunger and thirst mean? That we pray with all our hearts, all our souls and all our minds, praying fervently for miracles, especially spiritual miracles.

What does righteousness mean? That we pray for the will of the Father.

The rosary is an important spiritual weapon at all times, but especially when we have challenges with our family members. Pray by using the rosary in defense against evil and as a critical tool of healing. Whenever we call on the Blessed Mother to participate in the process, great healings can occur.

I pray a decade of the rosary daily for every member of my family for spiritual healing.

Every single day. When we pray in obedience for spiritual breakthroughs, we will see spiritual miracles. We also remember miracles occur in God's timing.

One of the most incredible spiritual miracles I've experienced occurred on my first trip to the Philippines. Our team visited the prison in Cebu, where Michael Jackson had filmed some of the music video 'Thriller."

As a help to their rehabilitation, the inmates are taught to dance together to rock songs. They work in unison on their dance steps.

One evening when we were there, seven camera crews filmed the inmates' dances. After a while, I was asked to pray with the inmates as I stood above the yard in a second-story area.

The camera crews took a break, and a prison leader asked me to preach directly to the inmates in the yard. I was excited and couldn't wait to get out there! However, just as I was walking down the stairs to enter the yard, a typhoon hit!

If you know anything about the Philippines and rain, you know the downpours are incredible. Completely drenching, obscuring everything. I couldn't see my hand in front of my face. The warden looked at me and said, "I guess you can't go out there."

At that point the miracle really gets started. I had travelled 10,000 miles to see God's people in the Philippines. I had a dream in which I was commanded to go.

I even was going to resign from my job because my boss had refused five times to allow my trip. I went to see the Vice President of Human Resources, a devout Christian, and asked his opinion. He went to see his pastor who told him to pray. That night he had a dream and God told him, "You don't know what I have in store for Steve; let him go on the trip."

Back at the office, he found a way to help me go on the trip, without resigning. I had prayed and prayed for a miracle.

After all that had happened to allow this trip, I found myself looking at a typhoon just when I

had an opportunity to share the love of Jesus with more than 1,000 people.

I prayed fervently.

"Lord," I said, "You wanted me to go to this country to love your people. Now when I have this great opportunity, the weather is stopping me. I believe in you. I believe in your miracles. Tell me what to do."

I truly expected God to act and tell me something incredible. I wasn't disappointed. He told me to ask the warden, "Wait two minutes."

I looked at the warden in the eye and said, "Can we wait two minutes?" I could see the look in his eyes and sensed his obvious thoughts. "Two minutes. Who are you kidding? Have you seen the storm? A category-five typhoon?"

He stuttered, "Well, okay."

My brothers and sisters, what happened next I never will forget. In exactly two minutes, this category-5 typhoon ceased totally.

The warden looked at me and said, "I guess you can go out there."

I was so fired up, I burst outside. I was in the yard preaching for 30 minutes without a single drop of rain or gust of wind.

I began loving the inmates gathered there passionately with the love of Jesus, explaining Chapter 8 of Paul's letter to the Romans. These imprisoned men were not condemned by Jesus. All things work for good if they love Jesus and are called according to His purpose. Nothing will separate them from the love of Christ. They are adopted children of God. On and on. Pouring love out to them.

I could see the spiritual healing in their eyes. I could see how much they hungered to be healed and to give their lives to Jesus.

I asked them each to totally surrender their lives to Jesus. To surrender their hearts, souls, minds, pasts, presents and futures. Eight hundred men in the yard and hundreds more looking through windows above listened intently.

Every single one, and I mean every one, repeated the Sinners Prayer and gave their hearts and souls — their lives — to Jesus! They raised their arms in the air praising God. Incredible! Alleluia!

A year later, I learned that a delegation from the prison had gone to the worldwide Eucharistic Congress in Cebu the following January and proclaimed to the assembly that they each had given their lives to Jesus.

What a miracle! God's love is incredible. The more we bask in it and draw upon it, the more miracles occur!

Chapter 15
Physical Healing

Physical healing has been the most common request in my 40 years of experience in ministry to God's people. So many are in physical pain and look to God for healing.

The most important aspect of praying for any type of healing is to pray with the love of Jesus. My prayer always is, "May it be all of You and none of me." That is when miracles start happening. When I pray over people, I pray to be the vessel of the love of Jesus Christ.

Healing for Mother and Baby

An example of the power of healing prayer can be demonstrated through the story of a woman who I worked with for several years. One day she told me that she was expecting her second baby.

She said to me, "I'm scared because I had a significant problem-pregnancy with my first child, and I am concerned about what is going to happen now."

As she spoke to me, I immediately felt the presence of the Holy Spirit. I saw in my spiritual vision how much God loved her.

Every single time I worked with and saw her after she had shared her worries, I prayed over her. I prayed for the love of Jesus to flow through her and flow through her pregnancy and her child.

With her first baby, the woman had problems leading up to the birth, and she was unable to take the baby to full term. With this pregnancy, she literally worked up until the day of her Cesarean-section surgery.

In the delivery room, as she was delivering the baby, the doctor suddenly gasped loudly. That's not something you want hear from the surgeon during a surgery.

Later, the woman found out the doctor gasped

because the uterine wall was so thin, she and the baby should have died. But, praise God, not only was the baby in perfect health and blessed, the mother suffered no harm as well! God is so good! All the time!

A week later, when I was asleep and dreaming, the Lord showed me all the locations and times of my prayers over my colleague and how those prayers had protected her and the baby. God wants us to believe. He wants to heal us according to His perfect will.

A most important lesson of healing is found in Chapter 9 of Matthew's Gospel—the story of the two blind men.

Jesus asked the men if they believed he could heal them. He then told them that the extent to which they believe is the extent that they would be healed.

I believe God asks us the same question. "Do you believe?"

Healing a Woman Who Believed

Another encounter with physical healing that I have experienced occurred on one of the pilgrimages Mary Anne and I lead as part of our ministry, Spirit Filled Hearts. Often these pilgrimages travel to the Holy Land.

On one trip, a woman, who was an internal-medicine physician, developed all the symptoms of the flu. She had a high temperature, chills and sweating and she told me that she should go to the hospital. I knew that as a physician, she obviously could diagnose her own situation. However, I also knew that God is the God of miracles.

We were riding in a bus over sacred ground in the Holy Land, and I felt the Holy Spirit come upon me.

I asked the woman if she wanted to be healed, the same question Jesus asked of the crippled man at the pool of Bethesda (John 5:1-18). She said, "Yes."

I then asked if she believed that Jesus could heal her, the question Jesus asked of the blind men in Matthew's Gospel (9:27-30). The woman looked at me and said she believed. Everyone on the bus began praying fervently for her, praying in tongues, singing songs, believing in a miracle for the woman. By the time we returned to the hotel, the sweats, chills and fever had disappeared. The big smile on her face said everything—completely healed!

I could tell she was truly sincere when she stated her belief in God's healing power. Her faith, belief and her love of Jesus supported the prayer for immediate healing.

Healing of Eye Disease

Another example of instant healing happened at a SCRC in Anaheim, California several years ago. On the Saturday evening of the weekend charismatic conference, Mass celebration was followed by a healing service.

After the Mass had ended, the celebrant asked the attending priests and deacons if they had received a word from the Lord. If so, they were asked to go the microphone and share what God had told them.

My heart was beating rapidly. God had told me to say that He was healing eye disease. On the way to the microphone, the Lord clarified what I was to say. He wanted me to share a more specific affliction — macular degeneration, a serious disease in which one's vision becomes severely narrowed and which is very difficult to treat.

I went to the podium and, with great faith and courage, I pointed at the thousands in the audience and said that God was healing macular degeneration of individuals in several particular locations of the arena. I pointed straight ahead, to the left of center and to the far end.

The next day, the celebrant priest came running up to me. He related that three women who had been in the audience came to his booth and told him they were instantly healed of their macular degeneration when I prayed!
God is so good! God is so loving. We must learn to ask and believe. To seek and find.

Healing Through a Stand-In

One final example of physical healing illustrates how we can "stand in" and pray for healing of other people, especially people we love most dearly. God uses the love of the person praying to help in the healing process.
A woman who deeply loved her aunt approached me at the end of our prayer meeting and asked if she could "stand in the gap" for her aunt. The aunt was in critical condition having suffered a brain aneurysm. The doctors didn't know if she would survive.

We prayed fervently for the aunt's complete healing. Exactly two days later, she walked out of the hospital, completely healed!

God wants to heal us because He loves us. I know this is so because of the many healings of physical ailments I have seen, including blindness, paralysis, cancer, cardiovascular disease, depression and nearly every illness imaginable.

Jesus told us we will accomplish what He did in His ministry on Earth and more! He told us t to lay hands on the sick, and they will recover.

Do it! Do it with love! Do it with the love of Jesus! Expect and experience miracles!

Chapter 16
Environmental Miracles

In praying for miracles, I constantly desire to be in communion with God. We are told:

> "Pray without ceasing."
> *1 Thessalonians 5:17*

To me, that instruction means to be in constant awareness and communion with Jesus.

In John, Chapter 15, we read about the vine and the branches. We must be connected with Jesus to bear any fruit at all. An especially significant verse is:

> "If you remain in me and my words remain in you, ask for whatever you want and it will be done for you." *John 15:7*

When we are "one" with Jesus, we can ask anything of him and expect an answer. This

communion with Jesus was in my mind when I asked Him to calm the typhoon in the Philippines.

Another miracle that involved wind as well as fire occurred in Glendale, California, where I grew up—a terrain thick with brush. All too often, especially when the "Santa Ana" winds blow in from the desert and it's been a dry year with little, if any, rain, wild fires threaten the area's homes, structures and surrounding hills.

Such a fire occurred a few years ago. I was visiting my parents' home as a tremendous wild fire was moving toward the neighborhood with 50-mph-plus wind gusts and flames jumping 30-40 feet in the air.

I was out in front of the house trying to water down the roof when a firefighter approached and told me that a number of homes had burned completely already, and the firefighters had lost control over the fire. I was instructed to evacuate the area at once.

I began praising God and believing in His miracles, knowing that He is the God of all

creation, the God of fire and wind, and that with God, all things are possible. Just as God controlled the wind on the Sea of Galilee, I asked Him to stop the wind and the fire.

I did evacuate, leaving the house at 7 p.m.
The next morning, I drove back to my parents' home and, much to my surprise, the house was unharmed, and no other homes had burned beyond those that had been ravaged the previous afternoon.

I called over a firefighter and asked about what had happened the evening before. He replied that an amazing thing had occurred. Although they had not expected it, the wind suddenly shifted direction and burned out itself. This happened at the exact time of my prayer — 7 p.m. All the remaining homes were untouched by fire. The firefighter could not explain the totally unforeseen shift in wind direction.

Praise God! Now and forever!

Still another example of God's miracles in nature was a multiplication of paint that occurred on a Christian service mission to

Mexico. An organization in Tijuana, Mexico, a city just across the border near San Diego, California, builds small, one-room homes for the very poorest of the poor.

On one such build, I was in charge of the paint team. We were shorted several cans of paint from the supplier, and our task was to paint the interior of the home. All that remained in the paint can when we began our job was a sticky goo. The volunteers came up to me and asked, "What do we do, Deacon?"

Remembering Jesus' miracle of the multiplication of fish and the loaves, I asked God to multiply the paint! I instructed the volunteers, "Add water." Pouring water into the can, the seven volunteers began painting.

My eyes widened in surprise; the paint color and thickness was the same as the paint used on the exterior of the house. After we ran out of paint again, they asked me once more what to do.

I answered, "Add more water!"

When we had finished the interior, the color perfectly matched the exterior paint. Praise God now and forever!

God tells us over and over to trust Him. To believe. To know in our hearts and souls that He loves us. To ask Him for a miracle as a child would ask a parent.

Try it and expect and experience miracles!

Chapter 17
Emotional Miracles

Jesus wants to heal us body, soul and spirit. A significant part of our everyday healing process in the pursuit of holiness is emotional or mental healing.

I was in the pharmaceutical industry for 45 years, mostly as an executive, selling products for all different types of mental disease. I found the illness of depression one of the most debilitating challenges for so many people, including myself, over the years.

Many people think depression is not a disease or they simple don't believe God is capable of healing it. But Jesus can and does heal everything! We must trust him and ask for healing!

It is also important to recognize how and when

Jesus comes to heal us.

When I was much younger, and our children were small, I was very successful and had been promoted to a Director-level position at age 32, the youngest director in the company. I was in charge of Training and Development in the home office on the East Coast.

I let this professional success go to my head, becoming arrogant and neglecting to put God ahead of my own desires for power, fame and the world's temptations.

My family was in disarray when, sometime later, I was promoted again and we moved back to California. Before moving east, I had headed up a thriving prayer meeting, for seven years had run a Christian Service program to feed the poor and was extremely active in church.

When I returned to Southern California, I didn't want to go to church at all, let alone do anything to help people. I wanted to curl up in my bed and never leave. I didn't want to talk to anyone.

One day at church, a very saintly man, Chris

Hickey, the person in charge of Eucharistic Ministers (EM), asked if I wanted to be an EM. I saw in his request an invitation from Jesus. God had not given up on me! I said yes, and the healing process started.

That year I again attended the SCRC at the Anaheim convention center. I was seated on the floor of the arena while a music group was singing, "You are Near."

Suddenly a miracle occurred. God rushed upon me and showed me one image after another of my life: feeding the poor, ministering to the sick, evangelizing people who didn't know Jesus and on and on.

While the experience lasted only about 30 seconds, it had a lifetime effect on me. God clearly told me in a voice that rang through my head, "This is how I see you."

God doesn't see the garbage. As Romans says,

"Now there is no condemnation for

those who are in Christ Jesus." *Romans 8:1*

Jesus died on the cross for <u>our</u> sins. He wipes them clear when we repent and confess our sins.

I am totally convinced the Sacrament of Reconciliation is the basis and foundation of mental healing. However, the devil continues to battle against our repentance, trying to convince us that we are worthless. Don't let him in the door. Commit to memory the verse from 2 Corinthians:

> "Take every thought captive in obedience to Christ." *2 Corinthians 10:5b*

Mary Anne and I learned a very important tool to combat the Devil's temptation to thoughts of worthlessness. When negative thoughts enter our minds or someone says something that can bring us down emotionally, we say silently or out loud, "I don't receive that!" Try it; it works!

Paul's epistle to the Philippians contains important guidelines regarding God's healing of mental health.

"Rejoice in the Lord always. I shall say

it again: rejoice! Your kindness should be known to all. The Lord is near. Have no anxiety at all, but in everything, by prayer and petition, with thanksgiving, make your requests known to God. Then the peace of God that surpasses all understanding will guard your hearts and minds in Christ Jesus.

"Finally, brothers, whatever is true, whatever is honorable, whatever is just, whatever is pure, whatever is lovely, whatever is gracious, if there is any excellence and if there is anything worthy of praise, think about those things...Then the God of peace will be you."   *Philippians 4:4-9*

Memorize these critical verses when asking God's healing and miracles for mental and emotional health. No matter what has happened, God is here to love and heal you!

Sometimes God gets our attention in other ways, using our emotions to demonstrate His love through a miracle event.

One such time occurred at Newport Beach, California. Mary Anne and I were sitting on our beach chairs watching the sand and the ocean. We noticed a group of young adults who had been playing volleyball had stopped to search the sand.

At first we saw a young woman combing through the sand, then followed by one friend after another. The group of five were all examining the sand, looking for something.

Mary Anne kept nudging me to get up out of my comfortable chair and help them, but I did not comply. Almost 30 minutes went by and still nothing was found.

Finally, my wife said, "DEACON!" That did it!

I asked the Lord to guide me. He quickly came to me and said, "The woman has lost something so that she may learn how much I love her."

I approached the young woman and asked what had happened.

She replied, "I lost something very precious to me, the watch my mother gave me."

She pointed about 25 yards away where her friends continued to search in the sand and said, "I think it is in that area." She then walked back to join them.

I will remember always the miracle that occurred next. The Lord told me the watch was five steps to the right of me. I took the steps and, in a few seconds, found a watch lying on top of the sand, not covered by a bit of sand. The sun was shining on the face of the watch, like a spotlight or the star in a Nativity scene.

Wow!!! How could they have missed it? Because God had blinded their eyes.

I took the watch, concealing it in my hand, and walked over to the young woman. Opening my hand, I asked if the watch was the one she had lost. She started crying.

I then asked her, "Do you go to church?"

She looked at me and said, "I will now!"

God is so good. He uses every means possible to capture our attention.

I witnessed another emotional miracle when I was a volunteer hospital chaplain. I visited hospital rooms, prayed with patients and gave them copies of religious prayers.

Each room's paperwork indicated if the patient wrote down a religion, so it was easy to find the Catholic patients. Normally, I only had enough time to visit just them.

However, on one particular day, God stopped me and told me to go into a room of a patient listed as a Muslim.

I said, "You sure Lord?"

"Yes!" I entered the room and found a female

patient with her brother sitting in a chair against the wall.

I asked her how she was doing and she answered that she was doing horribly because, she said, "I killed my husband."

Yikes! I wasn't sure if I wanted to thank God

for this assignment! (Just kidding.) I earnestly asked for the Lord's help.

The woman's brother offered me his chair to sit down.

I said, "No, I don't think so."

He looked at me and responded, "You're going to need it."

The woman explained that she had picked up her husband late at night at the airport in Los Angeles and asked him if she could drive him home. Her husband said "No."

Obediently, she, her mother and the woman's two children settled in the passenger seats. All fell asleep, including her husband. There was an accident. The woman's husband was killed, and the rest of the family landed in the hospital with many injuries.

Clearly she blamed herself for the accident.

I asked the woman if I could pray over her. She grabbed the Sacred Heart of Jesus prayer card

out of my hand, and I began to pray in the name of Jesus for a miracle and her healing.

The next week, I saw her again and she told me the night I first visited her, she later had a dream in which her husband appeared to her dressed in white. He told her that he was okay and that she and the family would be fine. She was beaming and praising God! God wants to heal us emotionally and give us blessings to heal our emotional wounds.

When we are most down, the dawn is coming soon. Expect and experience His wondrous love and miracles.

Chapter 18
Miracles through Evangelization

When we say "Yes" to Jesus, the Holy Spirit empowers us. Mary experienced the Spirit's empowerment during the Annunciation, when the Angel Gabriel tells her:

> "...'The holy Spirit will come upon you, and the power of the Most High will overshadow you...' "   *Luke 1: 35*

What happens when the Holy Spirit is released in us? Just before His Ascension into heaven, Jesus explained to His disciples:

> "But you will receive power when the holy Spirit comes upon you, and you will be my witnesses in Jerusalem, throughout Judea and Samaria and the ends of the earth." *Acts 1:8*

I have found when we say "Yes" to the Holy

Spirit, everything changes. We are compelled to share the Good News of Jesus with others. When that evangelization happens, God's miracles flow dramatically.

The Woman on the Plane

One evening on a flight from New Hampshire to Philadelphia, I was sitting in a window seat next to an empty center seat. A woman occupied the aisle seat. I felt the Lord's presence in a profound way, instructing me to talk to the woman.

I was reading my Bible, the flight was late at night, and I was tired. I resisted at first, but suddenly I sneezed. The woman looked at me and said, "God bless you!"

I felt a "bell" sound off. I turned to the woman and asked, "Are you going home?"

"Yes," she answered. "Yes. I am going home to see my husband and daughter. They think I was at a business conference, but I was with my lover."

Oh my! In seconds, the reality of the miracle about to happen became apparent.

I looked up to the sky and asked the Lord, "Why have You gotten me involved in this conversation?"

I had no idea what to say. I prayed for words from the Holy Spirit to guide me.

I said to the woman, "Tell me more about what has happened."

The woman explained her belief that cheating on a spouse was a normal and common behavior.

She looked at my Bible and said, "I see you are a Christian; so am I. However, Jesus doesn't expect us to be perfect. This is just my vice."

Hard to believe. She didn't know me, yet she is pouring out intimate details of her life. The Holy Spirit at work!
I prayed more. Then I looked at her and smiled

and asked this question: "Does the relationship with your boyfriend bring you closer to God?"

She looked at me and her eyes widened.

"Interesting you should ask that," she remarked. "I never pray with my boyfriend, but pray often with my husband."

I said, "One more question. Does this relationship bring you closer to your husband?"

She looked at me with tears in her eyes and said "This is so much like Jesus."

She explained between her tears, "Jesus doesn't come at you with a brick, but with a feather. You are my feather."

At that point, the landing gear was down, bells were going off, and I am holding her hand, leading her through a "Sinner's Prayer." She told me she planned to leave her boyfriend and return totally to Jesus and her husband! Praise God! Now and forever!

Jesus will use you 100 percent of the time you

are willing to be used—with power and miracles. Again and again.

The Garage Manager

One day while driving, one of my car's tires went flat. I was grumbling and complaining as I pulled into a gas station. I left the car with the garage manager and waited not so patiently at a nearby table. As often happens, the Lord's purpose became apparent.

I felt Him saying to me, "I have allowed this flat tire so that you can tell the garage manager how much I love him. Go to him."

I resisted for a minute and said, "You sure, Lord?"

Then I walked over to see the garage manager. I told him I was the Deacon at the local church and asked him, "Are you Catholic?"
He said, "Yes."
I whispered, "Whew."

Then he let loose the bomb. "But I haven't been to church for 30 years."

He added, "I have felt something in me to go back and take my family to church."

I explained to the man, "I was sitting waiting for the tire to be done when I felt the Lord instructing me to tell you how much He loves you. That you are forgiven. That the Lord is waiting for you with open arms."

Bingo. The man looked at me with eyes wide open, tears streaming down his face. He declared his intention to return to church the next weekend. Praise God!

Jesus constantly is looking for us to evangelize, which means in Greek to tell the "good news."

Our Good News is the foundation of God's love for us in so many ways. It must be proclaimed, and we must be the messengers. We must be open to His calling and guidance.
God's calling and guidance can come anytime and anywhere— in restaurants or stores, on

airplanes, in the streets, outside of church, even at sporting events! Every time I am called, I feel God's miracles and the presence of the Lord!

The Man in the Philippines

A recent Spirit Filled Hearts ministry trip to the Philippines was amazing. We ministered to thousands of people and were blessed to be allowed to conduct a healing service in Cebu at the Basilica of Santo Nino.

With thousands in the audience, the Lord came upon me.

I went to the microphone and said, "There is someone in the audience who is planning to kill himself tonight. The Lord is saying He loves you passionately and has forgiven you and to forgive yourself. Turn to Him, and he will bless and heal you."

At the end of the service, the celebrant of the Mass, a holy local Augustinian priest, approached to me looking as if he had seen a ghost.

He said to me, "A man came up to me at the end of the healing service and told me he was the man you had called out. He was planning on killing himself at the end of the service, but now he knows he is loved and will not harm himself."

Over and over again. When we say yes to Jesus, we will be used to love His people — to spread the Good News of Jesus Christ. When we say "Yes," we can, 100 percent of the time, expect and experience miracles!

Chapter 19
Miracles of Intervention

God uses angels, other people and every possible means to impact our lives.

I am convinced angels often appear to us if we are given the grace to see them, as Hebrews tells us.

> "Do not neglect hospitality, for through it some have unknowingly entertained angels." *Hebrews 13:2*

When our children were very small and our parish church hadn't been built yet, our Sunday Mass was celebrated in the local high school multipurpose room. One Sunday, the children were making a lot of noise, and we stood against the back wall to quickly take them outside if they got distractingly loud.

I was feeling very depressed about my

children's behavior and my skills, or lack of them, as a father. During the "Our Father," we held hands as a family, my left hand grasping my wife's hand. My right hand was free and I held it in the air. Suddenly, a woman grasped my right hand.

Where did she come from? She hadn't been standing near us. The woman squeezed my hand firmly. My eyes were closed, but I decided to open them to look the person holding my hand.

I saw a woman I didn't know, whose appearance was different. Her eyes were on fire with love, with peace, with joy — all at once. Her smile was wide and loving, and her eyes penetrated me to the core of my being.

It was as if she was saying, "Don't give up. You are loved. You are protected by God. Stay the course."

I put a big smile on my face and closed my eyes. Toward the end of reciting the Lord's Prayer, I realized no one was holding my right hand any longer. I looked up. The woman was nowhere

in sight.

I was standing by the hall door and quickly opened it to look down the long hallway in both directions. No one was there; but it had only been a few seconds. Was the woman an angel?

Well, like most miracles, the question can be debated. For me, however, there was no doubt. She could not have disappeared so quickly if she were human. To this day, I have never experienced a look as intense as hers, touching me at the core of my soul. She gave me a message of love. A message of hope.

The Miracle on the Train Track

A friend of mind grew up by railroad tracks with a bridge spanning a deep valley. He often walked on the bridge tracks when he thought no train was coming.

One day he was on the bridge, not paying

attention, when he heard a loud voice, "Look behind you." My friend turned around and saw a train traveling fast, directly toward him.

He had no choice but try to reach the side of the tracks and hang on without being run over or falling down into the valley.
Truly a miracle happened that day. My friend reached the side of the tracks in time and pulled himself to safety.

To this day, he knows the voice had to have been that of an angel because he was all alone, no other person in sight. That intervention saved his life.

A Friend's Call

My final example of miracles through intervention occurred when a friend was told by the Lord to phone me immediately.

I had just found out terrible news about one of my children, and I was totally distraught. The time was about noon. I was at a business meeting and I did something I almost never did. I left the meeting to return to my hotel room.

Once inside, my cell phone rang. It was my friend. Coincidently, he was also on a business

trip, but he was in Paris, France. It was 9 p.m. in Paris.

He told me God had given him a message to call me immediately and tell me that everything would be fine.

Incredible! Once again—a miracle or just a coincidence? For me, definitely God's intervention. A miracle!

Trust in Jesus and expect and experience miracles!

Chapter 20
Intercessory Prayer and Miracles

Blessings and miracles happen so very often. For certain miracles, the direct laying of hands on a person is not always necessary. Miraculous power can also be a part of intercessory healing prayer.

To understand and embrace that we often intercede for other people in their lives is extremely important as we pray over them.

A gentleman, an infrequent visitor to our prayer group, showed up at one of our prayer meetings. He came to pray for his brother who had cancer.

He told me, "Deacon Steve, my brother has stage-four cancer. It is inoperable, and there's nothing they can do."

I asked the man if he believed in God's healing power. He said "Yes," and I could tell he believed.

I began praying fervently in the Spirit, visualizing God's light and love entering his brother's body and soul. The prayer group members prayed fervently for his brother who lived far away.

A prayer said with love, faith and fervent intensity often makes the difference, more so than its length or special wording.

A few months later, I saw the man at a convention. He greeted me with a big smile.

"I am not sure you know what happened to my brother," he said excitedly. "You had prophesied that God had healed him. Shortly after we prayed, my brother went to the doctor and, praise God, there was no trace of cancer. He was completely healed!"

Praise God now and forever!

We know when God is present, when love is present, miracles happen. When we pray with

others as intercessors for healing, some type of miracle will happen — spiritually, emotionally, and/or physically.

When we are obedient, we can always expect and experience miracles!

Chapter 21
Don't Give Up!

Perhaps the biggest faith challenge we encounter is perseverance — the determination to continue trusting in God no matter how difficult.

The enemy constantly whispers to us to give up:

"Nothing is happening. Prayer doesn't work."

"God isn't real. If He is real, He won't answer us because He really doesn't like us all that much because of our sins. Because of what we have done in the past. For not being a better Christian. For being a loser. A failure."

All total and complete lies.

We know from the eighth chapter of Romans

that God does not condemn us, that nothing

can separate us from God's love. How do we know? God <u>died on the cross</u> to make us holy — to make us spotless before Him.

Meditating as often as possible on these critical verses from Ephesians provides hope and confidence:

"Blessed be the God and Father of our Lord Jesus Christ, who has blessed us in Christ with every spiritual blessing in the heavens, as he chose us in him, before the foundation of the world to be holy and without blemish before him. In love, he destined us for adoption to himself through Jesus Christ in accord with his favor of his will, for the praise of the glory of his grace that he granted us the beloved.

"In him we have redemption by his blood, the forgiveness of transgressions in accord with the riches of his grace that he lavished upon us. In all wisdom and insight." *Ephesians 1: 3-8*

Think about these verses. Adopted children of

God with every spiritual blessing! We have the power of the Lord to do His will and accomplish the purpose for which we were created.

I will say it three times:

"Don't give up! Don't give up! Don't give up!"

Do not give up on your husband. Do not give up on your wife. Do not give up on your children. Do not give up on yourself. Do not give up on your health or finances! Do not give up on being healed of your sinful patterns. Persevere!

For family, in particular, don't give up. Pray and expect miracles. So many times when I pray over people, the very first thing that comes to me is a message about a family. The devil attacks families.

God wants to heal families. God will act and will protect you. He will send legions of angels to protect you and your family.

Praise the Lord with all your heart, soul and

might. Trust and expect miracles and you will see them.

A powerful method of praying is to pray to the guardian angel of the person for whom you are praying. Then ask your guardian angel to pray with that person's angel as well.

Perseverance guarantees the expectation and experience of miracles.

Try to live these verses from Hebrews every day:

> "...do not throw away your confidence; it will have great recompense. You need endurance to do the will of God and receive what he has promised." *Hebrews 10: 35-36*

When we believe, when we are unafraid, when we have faith, we can expect and experience miracles routinely, perhaps even daily. Our loving, compassionate God has promised us so.

Final Thoughts

God wants us to believe as little children. To have a child's trusting faith. To open our hearts to the love of the Father. It is this faith and openness that triggers miracles.

Miracles are love in action. Miracles are God's declaration that He will never leave us orphaned. We are His beloved.

During the course of this book, we have explained that God's miracles flow like a river. Open your heart and see them daily. It will change your life forever!

I will pray fervently for you forever!

In the abundant love of Christ,

Deacon Steve

Made in the USA
San Bernardino, CA
07 November 2017